My English Class

My ESOL READERS

Set One: Book 3

My English Class
My ESOL Readers: Set One: Book 3
ISBN: 978-1-84231-382-4

Text by Rama Rangan
Edited by Bethan Bligh
Illustrations by Lucy Massey

Text copyright © 2025 Rama Rangan
Illustrations copyright © 2025 Gatehouse Books
All rights reserved

First published and distributed in 2025 by Gatehouse Books
Printed by Short Run Press, Exeter, Devon, UK

British Library Cataloguing-in-Publication Data:
A catalogue record for this book is available from the British Library

No part of this publication may be reproduced in any form or by any means, electronic, mechanical, photocopying, recording or otherwise, without the prior written consent of the publishers.

I am Maria.

I learn English at Warrington and Vale Royal College.

I come to college once a week. I have classes in the morning and afternoon.

There are many students in our class.

They come from different countries.

I come from Poland.

I speak Polish and a little English.

My friends come from Iran, Iraq, Ukraine, Bulgaria, Sudan and other countries.

We all speak different languages.

In class, we speak English.
At break and lunchtime, we meet
in the café. We buy drinks and food
and eat there.

We speak with our friends
in English or in our languages.

We have a nice classroom.

There are many tables and chairs.
There is a big whiteboard
to write on.
There are many boards
with pictures, posters and our
written work.

There is a desktop computer
on our teacher's desk.

There is a smart board,
where we watch video clips
and listen to people talk in English.

Our teacher helps us
to speak English.

We have many speaking
and listening activities in class.

We also learn to read books
and write words and sentences.

We often play word games in class.

We have fun, but we also learn to speak, read and write in English. We enjoy our English class a lot.

We look forward to seeing our friends every week.